WELCOME TO SCONE PALACE

In the 400 years since my family first lived at Scone, the place has meant many things to many people. Great ceremonies and affairs of state have been conducted here. Generations of Murrays have made it their family home. It continues, as it always has done, to provide a secure livelihood for many who live locally. And today it also offers a unique first-hand experience of Scotland's heritage to the thousands who visit us each year.

It is hard to say precisely what is the essence of Scone. Partly it's the Gothic splendour of the palace itself and the tranquillity of the wooded grounds. Partly it's the fine possessions - the porcelain and ivories, the furniture and paintings - treasured not only for their intrinsic value, but as a record of our long and distinguished family history. Partly it's the surrounding estate, which we strive to maintain as an unspoiled and beautiful stretch of Scottish countryside.

But most of all, I believe, Scone is a community - a community that includes the people who work in the palace, who tend the grounds, who keep the estate running, and of course us, the family, who live here. We all have our roles to play in cherishing and preserving this priceless piece of Scotland's heritage. You, the visitor, have an equally important part to play in our community, and we are glad to welcome you.

Contents

The Place of Kings

Scone is a place that breathes history like nowhere else in Scotland. Today, in the 21st century, it is the home of the Earls of Mansfield, and a major attraction to visitors from all over the world. Fifteen hundred years ago it was the capital of a Pictish kingdom and an important seat of the ancient Celtic church. In the intervening centuries it has been the home of parliaments and the crowning place of kings. It has housed the Stone of Scone and been immortalised in Shakespeare's Macbeth.

Poised above the River Tay, Scone overlooks the routes north to the Highlands and east through Strathmore to the coast. The Grampian mountains form a distant backdrop, and across the river stands the city of Perth. Two thousand years ago the Romans camped here, at the northern limits of their empire. They never defeated the warlike Picts, the 'painted men', who later came to rule from Scone. But the followers of St Columba had more success. By the early 7th century a group of early Christians, the Culdees or servants of God, had established themselves here.

The First Council

The Picts were ousted in 843 by Kenneth MacAlpin, King of the Scots, as he expanded his kingdom from the west. According to legend, he murdered the Pictish nobles at a banquet. He may also have brought with him the king-making seat, or Stone of Scone, and set it on Scone's distinctively shaped Moot Hill. It was certainly at Scone in 906 when King Constantine held the first recorded council here, forerunner of the great medieval parliaments that set the laws of Scotland at Scone until the 1450s.

As the centre of the Scottish realm, Scone became the focus of struggles for power. Macbeth and his mortal enemy, Malcolm, whose father had been killed by Macbeth's forces, both ruled here in the 11th century.

Edward I's placeman, John Balliol, took the throne at Scone in 1292, only to rebel against his patron four years later. In the resulting English invasion, the Stone of Scone was apparently seized and taken to Westminster. Not long after, in 1306, Robert the Bruce was dramatically crowned here with the blood of his rival, Red Comyn, whom he had killed in a church, still fresh on his hands.

The Abbey

During the Middle Ages Scone also gained importance as a religious centre. In 1114, Alexander I founded an Augustinian priory beside Moot Hill. Half a century later, in 1169, the priory was elevated to the status of abbey, as befitted a place where kings were made. At Scone in 1249, the seven year-old Alexander III became the first Scottish king to be crowned, rather than merely enthroned. And in 1329, a Papal Bull granted Robert the Bruce's son, David II, the right to be anointed with sacred oil as part of the crowning ceremony.

These were days of continuing conflict with England. In 1406 James I succeeded his father while still a hostage in London, and only took the throne after his release in 1424. Still suspicious of English intentions, his first Act of Parliament at Scone was to ban football in favour of archery practice. His son James II later banned golf for the same reason, on penalty of a fine of four pence.

James I's great-grandson, James IV was the last of the King of Scots to be crowned at Scone, in 1488. With him the seat of power shifted to Edinburgh and the newly built Palace of Holyroodhouse. The Reformation followed and in 1559 'a riotous mob from Dundee' marched on Scone Abbey. John Knox himself

The rebuilt Scone Palace in 1580. The original Abbey at Scone was destroyed by a riotous mob from Dundee in 1559.

intervened but the mob returned the following evening and burned it down. Twenty years later the lands of the ruined abbey were made over to the Ruthven family who repaired and rebuilt the abbey palace.

In 1581 Lord Ruthven was created 1st Earl of Gowrie, but in 1600 the family was disgraced for an alleged conspiracy against James VI; although who conspired and who was conspired against remains a matter of debate. In any event, Scone was taken from the Gowries and given to the king's cup-bearer, Sir David Murray of Gospetrie, as reward for his timely intervention in the affair. So Scone passed into the hands of the great family from which the Earls of Mansfield are descended.

The Last Coronation

In 1651, in defiance of Cromwell who already controlled the southern part of Scotland, Charles II became the last man to be crowned king at Scone. But within months he had been forced into exile. James Edward Stuart, the Old Pretender, had still less luck. In 1715 he came to Scone for his coronation, but was forced to flee to France before it could take place. By

the time of the next visit by a monarch, more than a century later, great changes had taken place at Scone. In 1803, the 3rd Earl of Mansfield began rebuilding the medieval house as a gothic palace. It was here, in 1842, that the 4th Earl and his family entertained Queen Victoria on her way to the Highlands. Since then, Scone has been visited by the late Queen Elizabeth, the Queen Mother, who was a childhood friend of the late Earl of Mansfield; her daughter, Queen Elizabeth II; and the Emperor of Japan and the King of Sweden.

Earl and Countess of Mansfield with HM Queen Elizabeth the Queen Mother.

Hon. James Murray and Lady Georgina Murray with the Empress of Japan.

The Mansfield family continue to live here today, preserving the Palace of Scone and its surrounding estate as a unique living testament to Scotland's heritage.

5

The Stone of Scone

The whereabouts of the Stone of Scone remains one of Scotland's most enduring mysteries. A symbol of great power, the Stone has been surrounded by intrigue from its earliest days. Even its origins are shrouded in legend and uncertainty.

The copy of the Stone of Scone which stands on Moot Hill.

Some people suggest that it was Jacob's Pillow, brought from the Holy Land, via Spain, Ireland and the West of Scotland, to arrive at Scone in the 9th century. Others believe it may have been a royal stone belonging to the Scots from Antrim, or the Picts from the north-east. It could even have been a Roman altar stone taken from the Antonine Wall. Wherever it came from, it was certainly in use at Scone as a crowning-seat between the 9th and 13th centuries, though there is as much confusion about its appearance as its provenance. Some contemporary accounts describe it as being hollowed like a chair or seat. Some say it was blackish or made of marble. Some say it was sculpted, some that it was carved. Others believe it was banded with metal and set with lifting rings at each corner. During its five centuries at Scone, the Stone was kept in the monastic church and only taken out to Moot Hill for enthronements. At first it may simply have been covered with embroidered cloth for the king to sit on. Later it would likely have been set into a wooden throne.

King David I and his grandson Malcolm, depicted at Scone upon the throne which encloses the Stone of Scone.
(Illumination from the Charter of Kelso.)

By now, as Shakespeare knew, installing the new king on the Stone had become the hereditary duty of the Earls of Fife, Chiefs of Clan MacDuff.

Edward I

When John Balliol rebelled in 1296, Edward I marched north and removed what he believed to be the Stone to Westminster. There he had it mounted in a throne-chair. And there it remained for the next 700 years, despite a brief but sensational disappearance in 1950, when a group of Scottish Nationalist students broke into Westminster Abbey on Christmas Day and spirited it back to Scotland. But after a couple of weeks it was returned to Westminster where it stayed until finally being brought to rest in Edinburgh Castle in 1996.

The Mystery Remains

Despite the return of this great symbol of Scottish nationhood, the mesmerising question still remains: is the stone in Edinburgh today the real one? Or did the monks dupe Edward, Hammer of the Scots, by handing over a fake all those centuries ago? And if Edward believed he had the real one, why then did he return to ransack Scone Abbey again two years later, in 1298? What we do know is that the stone now in Edinburgh is of old red sandstone, very similar to that from which Scone Palace is built. This could mean that the original Stone was locally quarried, perhaps by the Picts or perhaps by Kenneth Macalpin. But this theory contradicts most of the others about the Stone's origins. Nor does the red sandstone match any of the early descriptions.

Alternatively, it could mean that once the Abbot of Scone heard the English were coming, he hid the original and had a substitute made from local stone.

Edward's men would have been none the wiser, though the King himself may have had his suspicions. If this is so, the Stone on which successive kings and queens, including our present monarch, Elizabeth II, have been crowned since the 14th century is nothing but a copy.

Many attempts have since been made to find a hidden stone, and much has been written about its possible whereabouts. But despite a couple of 19th century 'discoveries', the identity and resting place of the real Stone of Scone remain a tantalising mystery to this day. And as a final twist to the affair, there is always the possibility that even if Edward did take the real Stone in 1296, the young Scottish Nationalists had it copied, and it was the copy that they left to be found by police at Arbroath Abbey in January 1951.

Ni fallat fatum Scoti quocunque locatum Invenient lapidem, regnare tenentur ibidem

As long as fate plays fair Where this Stone lies the Scots shall reign

So foretold the chronicler John of Fordoun in 1383. But where does the real Stone lie? That is the question.

The copy of the Stone of Scone outside of the chapel on Moot Hill.

7

Timeline

83-85 AD

Agricola, Roman Governor of Britain, marches out from Bertha, north of Perth, to defeat the Caledonians at the battle of Mons Graupius.

297

The Picts emerge as the leading power north of the River Forth. Scone becomes the capital of their kingdom, Pictavia. 7th century followers of St Columba, known as the Culdees or servants of God, establish a monastic community at Scone that will last for 500 years.

710

King Nechtan of the Picts decrees from Moot Hill that Easter should be observed according to the calendar of the Roman, not Celtic, Church.

843

Kenneth Macalpin, King of Scots, defeats the Picts to become ruler of all northern Scotland. It is said that he brings with him the Stone of Scone.

906

King Constantine II holds the first ever national council on Moot Hill. Here he affirms the laws of the Christian faith.

1040

 Macbeth becomes King of Scotland. Contrary to modern popular belief, he rules wisely and well for 17 years until he is slain by Malcolm III.

1114

Alexander I founds an Augustinian priory at Scone. The priory later becomes an abbey within the bishopric of Dunkeld.

1210

The first parliament is held at Scone. These parliaments continue to make the laws of Scotland until the 1450s.

1249

Alexander III becomes the first king of Scotland to be crowned on the Stone of Scone, rather than simply enthroned.

1292

 Edward I of England chooses John Balliol to take the crown of Scotland at Scone Palace.

1296

John Balliol rebels. Edward's troops force Balliol to surrender the crown and royal regalia, and remove the stone to Westminster.

1306

Robert the Bruce (Robert I) is crowned twice at Scone, first by bishops, two days later by the Countess of Buchan, sister of the Earl of Fife.

1329

Robert I's son, David II, becomes the first King of Scotland to be anointed with sacred oil as part of the crowning ceremony.

1390

Robert II is buried at Scone. Robert III is crowned at Scone.

1398

Robert III creates Scotland's first dukedoms, Rothesay and Albany, at Scone Abbey. Future kings' eldest sons now become Dukes of Rothesay.

1424

Released by the English 18 years after his father's death, James I is finally crowned at Scone. He bans football in favour of archery practice.

1488
James IV, 'the ideal Renaissance prince', takes the throne at Scone.

1559
Scone Abbey falls victim to the Reformation when, despite the intervention of John Knox himself, 'a riotous mob from Dundee pillage and burn it'.

1580
Scone Abbey lands are given to the Ruthvens of Huntingtower, who rebuild the abbey palace. Lord Ruthven becomes Earl of Gowrie in 1581.

1600
The Gowries are disgraced for their alleged conspiracy against James VI. Scone is given to Sir David Murray of Gospetrie, James's cup-bearer.

1604

Sir David Murray is created Lord Scone. He is later made Viscount of Stormont, a stewartry in the vicinity of Scone.

1651
Charles II is crowned at Scone. Within months he is defeated by Cromwell at the Battle of Worcester and forced to flee.

1716
Prince James Edward Stuart, the Old Pretender, comes to Scone to be crowned, but departs in haste at the approach of Hanoverian forces.

1745

On his way south with his army Prince Charles Edward Stuart, Bonnie Prince Charlie, stays in Lord Stormont's town house in Perth and visits Scone.

1776
William Murray, 4th son of the 5th Viscount Stormont is created Earl of Mansfield. He presides as Lord Chief Justice of England for 32 years.

1799
David Douglas, botanist, is born at Scone. He goes on to travel North America and discover more than 200 species of plants, the best known of which is the Douglas Fir.

1803
The 3rd Earl of Mansfield employs William Atkinson to start rebuilding the medieval house as a gothic palace that echoes the monastic original.

1805
Landscaping of the new palace grounds includes the removal of the entire village of Scone to a new site two miles away.

1842
Queen Victoria and Prince Albert visit Scone for one night on their way to the Highlands. Curling is demonstrated in the Long Gallery.

1939
Like many other large houses, Scone is requisitioned during the war by the Government. It becomes home to a girls' school and a number of Polish refugees.

1958
The house is reinstated as a family home.

1966
Scone Palace and its grounds are opened for the first time to the public.

The Family

The Murrays are one of the great families of Scotland. As soldiers and statesmen, ambassadors and lawmakers, they have for centuries been close to the heart of Scottish affairs.

Their forefather was *Freskin de Moravia*, a 12th century Flemish nobleman who was granted land in the area east of what is now Inverness. This region came to be known as Moray or Murray. From Freskin are descended both the *Earls of Mansfield* and the neighbouring *Dukes of Atholl*.

Sir David Murray, who was given Scone by James VI.

The Murrays had held land in the vicinity of Perth for several centuries when, in 1600, the Gowrie family's misfortune became their good fortune. As a result of the Gowrie Conspiracy, *Sir David Murray* not only received the lands of Scone Abbey but also, shortly after, the title Lord Scone.

In 1621 he was made Viscount Stormont, but he died without children and a complicated settlement allowed the titles to pass to another branch of the Murray family, who had recently been created Lords Balvaird. In 1658 they also took on the titles of Scone and Stormont.

The Jacobite risings of 1715 and 1745 were turbulent times for many Scottish families. The *5th Viscount Stormont*, who had declared his opposition to the Treaty of Union, played host to the Old Pretender for three weeks at Scone in 1760, for which he was later fined and jailed along with his son *David, the 6th*

Viscount. Undeterred, David's sisters entertained the Young Pretender at Scone thirty years later during the '45. His younger brother James, meanwhile, had become one of the Young Pretender's closest advisers in exile, being created Jacobite Earl of Dunbar in 1721.

But the most famous of this generation of Murrays was another brother, William, who rose from the English Bar to become Lord Chief Justice and one of the greatest of 18th century British judges. Famous for his oratory, the 'silver-tongued Murray' is known for having reformed court procedure and developed commercial law to keep pace with the expansion of the British empire. He was also known for ground-breaking and often unpopular judgements, such as his declaration that slavers had no rights over their slaves on English soil. During the Gordon Riots of 1780, the mob singled him out for his even-handed treatment of Quakers and Catholics and burnt down his house in Bloomsbury, then marched on Kenwood House in Hampstead, which he had bought from the 3rd Earl of Bute in 1754. The rioters were dispersed and the house remained.

The Earldom

William Murray was created *Earl of Mansfield* in Nottingham in 1776 and, again for complicated reasons of succession, Earl of Mansfield in Middlesex in 1792.

"Consider what you think justice requires, and decide accordingly. But never give your reasons; for you judgement will probably be right, but your reasons will certainly be wrong"

Advice given to a new colonial govenor by 1st Earl of Mansfield.

He died in 1793 without an heir and was succeeded by his nephew, the *7th Viscount Stormont*, who by then had retired following his own brilliant diplomatic career as

ambassador, first to Vienna and later to
Paris. The *2nd Earl's* many friends
included Queen Marie Antoinette
whom he first met when she was a girl
in Vienna, and later in Paris as the wife
of Louis XVI.

The *3rd Earl's* interests lay more in
architecture and landscaping than
statesmanship. In 1802 he employed
the architect William Atkinson to
begin the huge task of converting
Scone into a gothic palace. His son, the *4th Earl* made
a promising start in public life but all but abandoned it
on the death of his young wife after only eight years of
marriage. He nevertheless lived to the age of 92 and
ended up as Father of the House of Lords.

More recently, the *7th Earl* enjoyed a political career as
Member of Parliament for Perth before inheriting the
earldom in 1935. His son, the present and *8th Earl of
Mansfield*, began his career as a barrister, before turning
like so many of his forebears to politics. In 1973 he
became one of the first British members of the
European Parliament. In 1979 he was appointed
Minister of State for Scotland and in 1983, Minister of
State for Northern Ireland. In 1985 he left active
politics to take up the post of First Crown Estate
Commissioner.

Lord and Lady Mansfield were married in 1955.
They have three children and four grandchildren.

*7th Earl and Countess of Mansfield at the coronation
of HM Queen Elizabeth II.*

7th Earl of Mansfield by Philip de Laszlo.

*Viscount Stormont with his
first Salmon catch.*

Viscount and Viscountess Stormont with their family.

11

Freskin (son of Oleg), Lord of Duffus in Murray or Moray c.1130

From whom descends:

William Murray, 2nd fuedal Baron of Tullibardine. d. c.1459

Sir William Murray of Tullibardine d. 1524. Ancestor of the Earls of Tullibardine and Atholl, later Dukes of Atholl

Sir Andrew Murray — Hon. Margret Barclay, heiress of Balvaird

Sir David Murray d. c.1550 — Hon. Janet, dau. of 4th Lord Lindsay of the Byres

Sir Andrew Murray of Balvaird d. c.1573 — Lady Janet Graham dau. of 2nd Earl of Monrose

Hon. William Murray of Letter Bannachty in Strathearn d. c.1588 — Barbara Pitcairn

Sir David Murray of Gospetrie, 1st Lord Scone and Viscount Stormont, granted Scone 1604 d. c.1573 — Elizabeth Betoun of Creich

Daivd Murray of Letter Bannachty d. c.1627 — Agnes, dau, of Sir William Moncreiffe of that Ilk

Rev. Sir Anthony Murray 1st Lord Balvaird d. 1644 — Lady Elizabeth Carnegie, dau, of 1st Earl of Southesk

THE EARLS OF MANSFIELD

SPERO MELIORA
UNI EQUUS VIRTUTI

David, 2nd Lord Balvaird, succeeded in 1658 as 4th Viscount Stormont and 4th Lord Scone d. 1668 — Lady Jean Carnegie, dau, of 2nd Earl of Southesk

David, 5th Viscount Stormont and Lord Scone d. 1731 — Marjory Scott of Scotstarvet

David, 6th Viscount Stormont and Lord Scone d. 1748 — Anne Stewart

Hon. James Murray, Jacobite Earl of Dunbar

William, created 1st Earl of Mansfield in Nottingham,1776, and 1st Earl of Mansfield in Middx, 1792. d.1793 — Lady Elizabeth Finch Hatton, dau. of Earl of Winchilsea

David, 2nd Earl of Mansfield in Middx, 7th Viscount Stormont and Lord Scone succeeded his uncle in the earldom d.1796 — (2) Hon. Louisa Cathcart, dau. of 9th Lord Cathcart. She succeeded her husband's uncle as Countess of Mansfield in Nottingham. d.1843

David William, 3rd Earl of Mansfield in Middx. d.1840 — Frederica, dau. of William Markham, Archbishop of York

William David, 4th Earl of Mansfield in Middx., succeeded his grandmother as 3rd Earl of Mansfield in Nottingham in 1843. d.1898 — Louisa Carr Ellison, dau. of Cuthbert Ellison

Legend

Coronet of Earl

Coronet of Viscount

Coronet of Baron

William David, Viscount Stormont. d.1893 — Emily Lousia, dau. of Sir John Atoll MacGregor of MacGregor

William David, 5th and 4th Earl of Mansfield, succeeded his grandmother. d.unm. 1906

The Hon. Andrew David, killed in South Africa commanding the Lovat Scouts, 1901

Alan David, 6th and 5th Earl of Mansfield, d.1935 — Margaret, dau. of Sir Malcolm MacGregor of MacGregor

Mungo David Malcolm, 7th and 6th Earl of Mansfield, d.1971 — Dorothea, dau. of Hon. Sir Lancelot Carnegie, son of the 9th Earl of Southesk.

William David Mungo James, 8th and 7th Earl of Mansfield — Pamela Foster, dau. of Wilfred Foster, CBE

Lady Malvina Murray — 20th Earl of Moray

Lady Mariota Murray — Hon. Malcolm Napier, brother of 14th Lord Napier and Ettrick

Hon. Alexander David Mungo, Viscount Stormont — Sophia Ashbrooke, dau. of Biden Ashbrooke

Lady Georgina Murray — John Bullough of Culcreuch

Hon. James Murray

Hon. Isabella Murray

Hon. William Philip David Mungo Murray, Master of Stormont

Hon. Iona Murray

Hon. Louisa Murray

12

The Palace

David, 3rd Earl of Mansfield, chose not to follow his father or grand-uncle into public life. Instead, he turned his attention and energy to the family home in Scotland, which he inherited in 1796, aged nineteen. When not abroad, his father, the ambassador, had spent most of his time at Kenwood House in Hampstead. The house at Scone, some two hundred years old, was by now in a sad state of disrepair.

Scone Palace drawn by J.P. Neale and engraved by S. Fisher.

In 1803 young David Murray set about rebuilding the house as a grand Georgian palace. It cost him the enormous sum of £60,000 and took nine years to complete. His architect was William Atkinson, a pupil of James Wyatt, the master of gothic design. Atkinson planned that the new building would echo Scone's monastic origins. The Earl meanwhile was keen to preserve some of the medieval features within the new setting. But a breakdown of communications between Atkinson and his clerk of works resulted in much being lost, though not the original marquetry oak floor of the long gallery.

Nevertheless, the finished building with its imposing gothic exterior and splendid regency interior was greatly admired. Today Scone is regarded as one of the most outstanding Georgian gothic houses still remaining. It is also known, interestingly, as the earliest house of its period to be both gothic and asymmetrical in design.

The Tour

Visitors to Scone today see all the formal rooms and vaulted galleries on the ground floor, perhaps over half of the whole interior of the palace. The Gift Shop is also situated on the ground floor. The present family also have their apartments here. In the basement there are offices, the restaurants and food shop, where previously there were kitchens, larders, laundries and other centres of domestic activity. At its peak, at the time of Queen Victoria's visit in 1842, the palace would have bustled with some forty staff - twenty-eight to look after the house and twelve in the stables - as well as many more working in the grounds.

In addition to the architecture, William Atkinson was responsible for much of the decoration and furnishing, which only completed around 1820. He was lucky in this respect to have many of the treasures acquired in London and Europe by the 1st and 2nd Earls. These included portraits by Van Dyck and Reynolds, furniture by Boulle and Reisener, Robert Adam and Chippendale, clocks by Viner and Thomire, and porcelain from Sèvres and Meissen.

However, all this was substantially augmented in anticipation of the royal visit of 1842. The 4th Earl had furniture locally commissioned, as well as new silk damask panels for the drawing room walls, along with gilt mouldings and a velvet pile carpet. Improvements continued throughout the 19th century as new amenities became available. Four years after Victoria's visit the palace was lit for the first time with coal gas. Hot water was installed in 1859 and modern drainage in 1861.

After a number of minor fires, one of which caused a great stir at a dinner party, a new hydrant was installed in 1890 which threw an inch jet of water 100 feet into the air. Electricity finally arrived in the 1920s - although there are still parts of the house that it hasn't reached today!

But what is most interesting about Scone Palace, today in the 21st century, is that despite the presence of modern amenities it has undergone almost no significant alterations in the two hundred years since the major works undertaken by the 3rd Earl in 1803.

The Octagon

Past and present come together in the Octagon, which was formerly part of the medieval gallery and led into the King's room where Charles II slept the night before his coronation in 1651. Since Atkinson's redesign, this small but airy gothic hall has offered an attractive place to pause between the Long Gallery and Inner Hall. Flanking the roof light, the ceiling bosses are individually carved with birds, foliage, a crown and a serpent. The shape of the room is accentuated by the octagonal rosewood library table, made in the 1820s by the Scottish cabinetmaker George Bullock.

The Dining Room

On a September evening in 1842 the family and a handful of carefully chosen guests would have stood by respectfully, perhaps a little nervously, as Queen Victoria and Prince Albert made their way to the table for

dinner. There, with the porcelain, crystal and silverware gleaming in the light of candles and lamps, the Queen dined with her loyal Scottish subjects.

Dumb Waiter from the Dining Room.

The other guests on this great occasion were the Duke and Duchess of Buccleuch (the Queen's lady-in-waiting), the Duchess of Norfolk, the Earl of Aberdeen, the Earl of Liverpool, Lord and Lady Kinnoull, Lord and Lady Kinnaird, and the Prime Minister of the day, Sir Robert Peel.

As the evening wore on and the party relaxed, the 4th Earl might have taken a moment to congratulate himself on the splendid new doors, side tables, cabinets and Chippendale style chairs, all made of

Queen Victoria and the Prince Consort by Winterhalter.
by Courtesy of HM The Queen

19

oak from the estate and specially commissioned from Ballingalls of Perth. He might also have reflected on the huge expense and general turmoil caused to a number of noble Scottish families by Queen Victoria's new-found penchant for the Highlands.

In August 1842 he had written to his mother: '... *although as you may easily imagine that a Royal visit this year will be very inconvenient, yet it would be perfectly inhospitable for me to decline ... I have written to the Duchess [of Buccleuch, the Queen's lady-in-waiting] that I shall be proud to receive Her Majesty, and have begun my arrangements immediately.*'

These arrangements included security which, even in those days, could not be ignored. The Earl continues: '*My difficulty is being obliged to keep the visit secret or I could do ten times as much. I have been obliged to take Ballingall [the cabinet-maker] into my confidence otherwise my furniture would not have been ready.*'

The dining room has of course been the scene of many less formal occasions since Victoria's visit in 1842. It is still used today for private and public functions of all kinds. With its unique collection of European ivories, its portraits and clocks, its fine porcelain and bronzes, it is a room designed for entertaining on a grand scale.

Altogether there are some 70 pieces of ivory. Mostly collected by the 4th Earl, they come from Bavaria, Flanders, Italy and France. They are carved in elephant and walrus tusk, and date from the 17th century for ivory first started flooding into Europe from India and Africa, through to the 19th century.

The Dining Room's collection of European Ivories

Top left: Venus and Cupid.

Left: The Holy family.

Right: 18th century Bavarian farmer.

Opposite page: Cupid with Lion.

20

The Ante-Room

With its stained glass window and vaulted gothic ceiling, this little room shows William Atkinson's vision at its best, evoking the peace and space and contemplative atmosphere of the old abbey.

There is a strong echo of the past too in the small contemporary painting on wood of Sir David Murray, James VI's Cup-Bearer, Master of the Horse and Captain of the Guard. Sir David was awarded the lands of Scone in 1604 and so became the first Murray to live here.

His portrait stands on a nineteenth century bureau plat, whose elaborate inlay is the first example of the brass and tortoiseshell Boullework which features so prominently throughout Scone. The Ante-Room also boasts a clock by Burnfield of Perth, made in 1850, the only Scottish clock in the State Rooms.

One of a pair of Chinese Porcelain Baluster Vases.

William Murray, 1st Earl of Mansfield
by Sir Joshua Reynolds in 1776.

The Drawing Room

Although the 2nd Earl hardly ever lived at Scone, his influence is strongly felt in the Drawing Room. A distinguished diplomat, he served as British Ambassador to the court of the ill-fated Louis XVI of France. The treasures he later brought back with him from Versailles accentuate the Regency opulence of this magnificent room.

David Murray already knew the young Queen Marie Antoinette from Vienna, where he had previously served as Ambassador at the court of her mother, Empress Maria Theresa of Austria. Once he was at Versailles, their friendship grew. There is even a story that he taught her and her husband Scottish dancing, to the undoubted amusement of the French courtiers.

In token of their friendship, Marie Antoinette presented him with one of three writing desks commissioned to mark her marriage (*left*). Made by Jean Henri Riesener, the most famous cabinet-maker of his day, it is recorded in the *Garde Meuble* inventory of French royal furniture. Today it is the *pièce de resistance* of the Drawing Room at Scone.

The courtly feeling of the Drawing Room owes as much to the silk brocade wall coverings and the royal blue and gold monogrammed carpet as to the splendid furniture and paintings. Among the many rare and valuable items, the pair of console tables either side of the fireplace, mirroring images of one another, is an exceptional example of Boullework.

No 18th century British Embassy was complete without full-length portraits of the monarch of the day. The huge paintings of George III and Queen Charlotte, either side of the fireplace, are by Allan Ramsay, the young Scottish artist who became court painter to George III, and who also happened to be the 2nd Earl's cousin by marriage. Gazing down the length of the room are the 1st Earl of Mansfield and his wife, Elizabeth. Dressed in his Lord Chief Justice's robes, William Murray was painted by Sir Joshua Reynolds in 1776, the year he received the earldom. His wife was painted by another Scots artist, David Martin, from Anstruther in Fife. The more modern portraits of the 7th Earl and Countess, parents of the present Earl, were painted by Philip de Laszlo in 1932 and 1928 respectively. The Countess, Dorothea (*below*), is portrayed as a young woman shortly before her engagement.

Dorothea Carnegie, later wife of the 7th Earl of Mansfield
by Philip de Laszlo.

24

The Library

Once the conversion of the original building to gothic palace was complete, the 3rd Earl would doubtless have spent much time at his desk in this airy, spacious library, planning the landscaping of the grounds and the running of the estate.

This is perhaps the gothic room *par excellence* at Scone. Atkinson's designs are reflected in the doors and their surrounds, the glazed bookcases, the fireplace, even the Earl's ornate partner's desk with its gothic giltwork. Many of these items are made of oak from the estate.

Today most of the bookcases no longer hold books. In their place is an exceptional collection of family porcelain including pieces from Sèvres,

Meissen, Ludwigsburg, Chelsea, Derby and Worcester. It is remarkable now to think that most of these pieces would

have been acquired for everyday use.

William Murray, 1st Earl of Mansfield by Martin.

The 1st Earl's armorial service dates from before he was created Earl. It bears the Stormont arms and the family motto, *Uni Aequus Virtute, Friendly unto Virtue Alone*. As was the custom of the day, the 47-piece set was sent to China to be painted and fired.

The apple green and gold service by Sèvres is particularly unusual in colour. It is believed to have been a gift from Louis XVI, designed by the King and the 2nd Earl together; although neither would then have known that arsenic in the green paint made the service potentially lethal.

29

The Ambassador's Room

Allan Ramsay painted the 2nd Earl (displayed on the easel) in 1759 when he was still Viscount Stormont. He is portrayed as a man of openness and charm, qualities entirely fitting for a distinguished diplomat. He was known to be highly intelligent, and was much admired for his sharp wit and refined taste.

He was also evidently not averse to the more sumptuous trappings of office, such as the magnificent bed canopy, complete with royal coat of arms. This was converted from the two state bed canopies he would have had in his possession during his ambassadorships in Vienna and Paris.

There are a number of interesting portraits in this room. The palace-building 3rd Earl and his wife, both by Hoppner, hang either side of the fireplace. The 2nd Earl's sister-in-law, 'the beautiful Mrs Graham', sat frequently for Gainsborough. The Dowager Lady Mansfield, mother of the present Earl,

was painted by her godson Douglas Anderson, a pupil of Annigoni. But perhaps the most intriguing of all is the Zoffany portrait of Lady Elizabeth Murray. She is accompanied by an attractive young black girl who appears in the painting to be her attendant but was in fact her cousin and playmate, Elizabeth Dido Belle. Dido's natural father, Sir John Lindsay, a captain in the Royal Navy, was a nephew of the 1st Earl, as was Elizabeth's father, the Ambassador, later 2nd Earl. Both girls were being cared for at Kenwood by their mutual great-uncle, the Lord Chief Justice, who left Dido £500 and an annuity of £100 when he died in 1793.

The Lady Elizabeth Murray (daughter of the Ambassador, later 2nd Earl) with Dido, by Zoffany.

The Inner Hall

Like the Ante-Room, this long inner hallway also bears strong echoes of the cloistered, monastic feel of the ancient abbey. But there is nothing monastic about its contents, with the ornate Italian, French and Oriental furniture, the animal exhibits and paintings.

The two brown bears were shot by the Hon Sir Lancelot Carnegie, the present Earl's maternal grandfather, when he was secretary at the British Embassy in Moscow in 1908. The paintings of dromedaries and monkeys by the 17th century Flemish artist David Teniers, were

bought for the 3rd Earl in 1810 by William Seguier, the first Keeper of the National Gallery in London. Where the pair of elephant skulls came from, no one knows.

One of the brown bears shot by Hon. Sir Lancelot Carnegie while secretary at the British Embassy in Moscow.

Sir Lancelot later visited China where he acquired the imposing black lacquered cabinets. These house a fine collection of 18th and 19th century Japanese

and Chinese porcelain. The cabinets themselves incorporate panels from Chinese lacquered screens and

are complimented by a pair of black lacquered Regency chiffoniers in Brighton Pavilion design. At the far end of the hall stands a pair of late 18th century French Boullework marriage caskets.

Lapis lazuli cabinet.

Monkeys by David Teniers the Younger.

Orchids at Scone

A passionate grower of orchids, the present Earl of Mansfield has the largest private orchid collection in the country. Plants from Scone have won international awards and in 1990 an orchid was named *Phalaeonpsis* "Earl of Mansfield".

Since January 1986 there have been orchids in flower every day at Scone Palace. Today, the plants that adorn the state rooms are grown in a purpose-built orchid house.

'The Village Politicians'

The vulgar realism of David Wilkie's *The Village Politicians* caused a sensation when it was first shown in 1806. Commissioned by the 3rd Earl of Mansfield from the unknown twenty-year-old Scottish artist for the sum of 30 guineas, it was immediately acclaimed for the way it echoed the style of the 17th century Flemish artist David Teniers, in its portrayal of the inflammatory effects on the poor of drink, talk and newspapers.

The Long Gallery

As a visitor to the medieval house, first as guest of the Gowries, later of the Murrays, James VI would have strolled in this remarkable gallery which was then decorated with murals of hunting scenes, obligingly featuring James himself as the principal huntsman. These were sadly lost during the rebuilding, due to the misunderstanding between Atkinson and his clerk of works. But the gallery's extraordinary proportions remain – at nearly 150 feet (45 metres) it is the longest room of any house in Scotland – and the sense of history hangs palpably beneath its imposing fan vaulting.

Here Charles II walked in procession on the way to his coronation on Moot Hill. Here the Old Pretender, James Edward Stuart, awaited a coronation that was not to be. And here Queen Victoria and Prince Albert witnessed an indoor curling demonstration on the highly polished oak and bog oak marquetry floor, a relic of the earlier house dating from 1580. Following the display, Prince Albert agreed to become first president of the Royal Caledonian Curling Club.

On less formal occasions, family and guests would have used the gallery for taking exercise when the weather was poor. They might also have gathered for recitals on the magnificent organ that dominates the gallery's west end, a birthday gift from the 3rd Earl to his wife. Made in 1813 by Thomas Elliott, an English organ builder, and installed by a specialist from York Minster, it remains in its original condition apart from the addition of an electric fan. The organ is still regularly played at the weddings that are held in the Long Gallery.

Among the Long Gallery's many treasures, the most distinctive must be the unique collection of Vernis Martin vases and ornaments. The 70 pieces were originally part of a 120-piece set. The remaining pieces were bought by the Czar of Russia and housed at The Hermitage in St Petersburg until they vanished in 1917.

Vernis Martin is heavily varnished and highly decorated *papier mâché*. The technique was originally developed for producing, amongst other things, strong but lightweight panels for carriages and sedan chairs. The varnish was also used as a wall-covering for rooms. The technique was perfected in the 1720s, at the time of Louis XV, by the Martin brothers of Paris who used it to create a vast range of fashionable *objets d'art*.

Decorated by leading contemporary artists, embellished and mounted with silver and gold, the largest pieces in the Scone collection were designed so as not to be dwarfed by the palatial surroundings of Fontainebleu and Versailles. But such was the 18th century vogue for Vernis Martin lacquer that it ended up being applied to every conceivable object, no matter how small.

The Slip Gallery

On 6 September 1842, Queen Victoria would have made her way down this short hallway as she retired to the suite of rooms that had been specially prepared for her visit to Scone.

On her way she might have paused to glance at the Italian alabaster panels depicting the coats of arms of David Murray, the 1st Lord Scone, and his wife Elizabeth Betoun, whom he married in 1604. Carved by the same artist who created the monument in the Chapel, these were probably removed from the medieval building and installed in the Slip Gallery by the 3rd Earl.

*Lady Susan Murray
as a child.*

37

Queen Victoria's Suite

The Queen had requested ground floor apartments because she preferred not to sleep on an upper floor. These three pleasant south-facing rooms were duly converted into a boudoir for her, a bedroom, and a dressing room for Prince Albert.

Today the rooms have been rearranged. What was the Queen's boudoir now contains the bed, hangings and curtains, all specially made for the royal visit. What was the bedroom is now used for small private functions, decorated in a modern recreation of the colours and Scottish motifs popular at the time. The third room, Prince Albert's dressing room, now houses models of both the medieval house and the gothic palace, as well as maps, plans and letters connected with the rebuilding.

Needlepoint Firescreen showing the Royal Coat-of-Arms.

A commemorative display of the visit to Scone by Queen Victoria and Prince Albert.

The Lennox Room

This room is named after the Duke of Lennox who was the great friend of James VI, and so a frequent visitor to the medieval house in the days of the 1st Viscount Stormont. Its contents today are rich with royal associations.

The gateleg oak table is said to have belonged to James VI who presented it as a gift to his host. The oak armchair was used half a century later by Charles II when he came to Scone to be crowned.

It seems likely that the large wall hanging, showing *Justice* and *Mercy* embracing, was commissioned by *Mary Queen of Scots*, while the embroidered bed hangings were almost certainly worked by the Queen herself, together with her ladies, perhaps during her imprisonment in Loch Leven Castle.

Bed hanging worked on by Mary Queen of Scots, during her imprisonment in Loch Leven Castle.

40

The graveyard of the village of Scone.

The old cedars of Lebanon around the chapel on Moot Hill.

Abbey & Gardens

It is nearly nine hundred years since the Augustinian monks first began tending the land around their abbey. Today the abbey is gone and the grounds bear witness to the early 19th century vision of the 3rd Earl's landscape designer, John Loudon. But beneath the grass and among the trees, within sight of the palace, there are still many reminders of Scone's more distant past.

If you were to stand on what are now the front steps of the palace, the abbey would once have risen across the lawns before you. Beyond would have bustled the village of Scone, gradually sprawling out through the centuries until at its peak, in the 1790s, it had more than 1400 inhabitants. Ten years later, however,

The Mercat Cross.

it had disappeared completely, knocked down and rebuilt on its new site at New Scone, two miles away. Today only the Mercat Cross and graveyard testify to its existence. The nearby 16th century archway, meanwhile, is all that remains of the approach to the building.

The trees at Scone forge another strong link with the past, from the fine old cedars of Lebanon around the chapel, to the rare and exotic conifers in the 4th Earl's mid-19th century pinetum. There are no formal gardens at Scone, but the natural surroundings of the woodland gardens with their borders, flowering shrubs and trees create a delightfully peaceful setting for strolling or picnicking.

Avenue of Noble Firs in the 19th century Pinetum.

The 16th century archway.

47

David Douglas

Among the finest of all the trees at Scone is a giant Douglas Fir. It is prized not just for its size, but because it was raised from the first seed sent home from North America in 1826 by the man after whom it is named, David Douglas. This famous early nineteenth century explorer and botanist was himself a son of Scone.

David Douglas was born in the village of Scone in 1799 and worked as an under-gardener in the newly-landscaped palace grounds. He later went to work at the Botanical Gardens in Glasgow where his talent was quickly noticed and he was sent to North America as a collector for the Royal Horticultural Society. In the course of only a few years he sent back over 200 new species of plants. Lupins, phlox, sunflowers, californian poppy, mimulus, flowering currant and snowberry are just a few of the common plants he discovered. He is most famous though for the giant conifer which he initially named *Pseudotsuga menziesii* after its discoverer, Archibald Menzies of Aberfeldy, another Scot, who had sailed to the Pacific coast with Captain Vancouver.

Douglas travelled widely and adventurously, from Oregon to Hudson's Bay and even Hawaii, recording and collecting plants wherever he went. His journeys took him through unmapped forest and to the summits of previously unscaled mountains. After surviving many dangers he fell, in suspicious circumstances, into a pit that had been dug as an animal trap. Here he was tragically gored to death by a wild bison bull that had also fallen into the pit. He was only 36 years old.

A pencil sketch of David Douglas F.L.S. (1799-1834) by his niece Miss Atkinson.

by Courtesy of The Royal Horticultural Society

48

The Maze

Sculpture of Aresthusa in the centre of the maze.

The Scone Maze is designed in the shape of the five-pointed star that features in the Murray family crest, and appears as a motif throughout the palace. The maze comprises 2,000 beech trees, half of them green, half of them copper, planted in such a way as to create a unique tartan effect.

The Scone Maze is the work of contemporary maze designer, Adrian Fisher. It is 215 feet across and has at its centre a pentagonal fountain by sculptor David Williams-Ellis. In the early days of its growth the young beech trees proved irresistible to the local roe deer population, until they were eventually scared off by fragrant offerings from the lions of Edinburgh Zoo.

The site of the maze is the ancient area of flat ground known originally as the Monks' Playgreen. It was here, until the sacking of the Abbey of Scone in 1559, that the monks played their own version of football.

The maze on the monks' playgreen; from the air the different colours of beech tree can be easily distinguished.

49

The Estate

The LOGIEALMOND HILLS on the northern tip of the Scone Estate.

For all the weight of history that surrounds it, Scone Palace is also the hub of a large and thoroughly modern estate. Run as a family business, this combines the management of profitable farming, forestry and sporting activities with a commitment to high standards of conservation and environmental sustainability.

The estate's 33,000 acres include some of the finest arable farmland in Tayside, as well as some of its most spectacular sporting locations. Through its centre runs one of the world's great salmon rivers, the River Tay. At its northern edge, sheep graze the heatherclad Logiealmond Hills in the company of grouse and black game. In the neighbouring pine-woods are still to be found a handful of the huge, turkey-like capercailzie for which Tayside was once famous.

With nearly 2000 hectares of woodland, timber growing and sawmilling are also important estate activities. Commercial woodland management has been going on at Scone for more than 400 years, and David Douglas's legacy lives on in the estate nurseries. Fittingly enough, Scone oak is to be found today in the buildings of the new Scottish Parliament.

With its farmlands and woodlands, hills and rivers, Scone estate enjoys a particularly rich variety of wildlife habitats. Boxing brown hares frequent the lower lying farmlands, while their cousins, the blue or mountain hares, turn snowy white on the Logiealmond Hills in the winter months. Red squirrels are still to be seen in the woodlands, and sharp eyes may glimpse a kingfisher on the banks of the Tay. Roe deer betray their visits to the palace lawns by their tracks in the early morning dew.

Each July, Scone becomes the venue for one of the highlights of the Scottish countryside calendar, the annual Game Conservancy Scottish Fair. Then the parklands beneath the palace bustle with stalls and displays of country pursuits. Other annual events include the Scone Horse Trials, and Farming of Yesteryear, with its display of agricultural machinery and vehicles from a bygone age. The palace also has its own racecourse, where racegoers gather from spring to autumn for meetings of the Perth Hunt.

Hospitality

Like many large houses today, Scone Palace relies for part of its upkeep on the income derived from letting out its facilities. In recent years Scone has come to be known as a unique and highly prized venue for banqueting and conference events of all kinds.

From the grandeur of the State Dining Room to the intimacy of Queen Victoria's Room, the elegance of the Drawing Room and the spaciousness of the Long Gallery, each of the six main state rooms offers its own particular atmosphere for events of different kinds. These range from conferences and product launches to weddings and dinner parties, lectures and musical evenings.

Outside, with their spectacular views across the River Tay, the palace parklands are equally in demand for sporting activities. Corporate clients from all over the country bring staff and guests to Scone to enjoy outdoor pursuits that include archery, clay pigeon shooting and off-road driving.

Our Valued Visitors

Scone Palace is no stranger to visitors. Over the centuries, people have come here to attend coronations and parliaments, marriages and funerals, banquets and grand balls, shooting parties and race meetings. But our visitors have never been more highly valued than they are today. For without your interest, we cannot continue to preserve this unique living testament to Scotland's heritage. Wherever you began your journey - and many, we know, come from far-off places - we hope that you have enjoyed your visit. Perhaps it's the sense of history that has been of interest to you, perhaps the paintings and *objets d'art*, perhaps the Gothic splendour of the architecture, or the peace and calm of the wooded grounds. Whatever it is about Scone that has caught your imagination, we hope you will tell your friends about it so that we can welcome them when they come, as we sincerely hope to welcome you on your return.